Kindness
A to Z

Alphabet by HEART

by JEANNE & MARK K. SHRIVER

Illustrated by LAURA WATSON

4U2B
◄ BOOKS & MEDIA ►

4U2B
◀ **BOOKS & MEDIA** ▶

ISBN: 978-0-8294-5483-3
Library of Congress Control Number: 2023952194

The name of Best Buddies is reproduced with the kind permission of
Best Buddies International, Inc. www.bestbuddies.org BEST BUDDIES

4U2B Books and Media is an imprint of Loyola Press,
8770 W. Bryn Mawr, Chicago, IL 60631   4U2BBooks.com

Printed in the United States of America.
24 25 26 27 28 29 30 31 32 33 CGC 10 9 8 7 6 5 4 3 2 1

ABC

Letters make words; this much is true.
And there is no limit to what words can do.

Words have power to bring good or bad,
to make us happy or make us sad.

Which way will you go when you use the letters?
Will you make things worse or make things better?

Using kind words is a good place to start.
They're the best way to learn the alphabet by heart.

 **Aa**

I **admire** your art.
It's colorful and new!
I admire your art.
It's an expression of you.

Bb **Believe** in yourself and all that you are. Anything is possible when you shoot for a star.

Cc

Care about people,
not the things that you see.
When you care about people,
the happier you'll be.

Dd

It's exciting to **dream**,
whether asleep or awake.
Dreams are adventures—
fun journeys to take.

Ee Empathy tells others they are never alone. Imagine their feelings, and make them your own.

Ff You **feel** snowballs and sunshine.
That's a great start.
But the best things to **feel**
are the things in your heart.

Gg

Gratitude is happiness stirring about.
When you feel grateful, a big "Thank you!" pops out.

Hh

You'll feel like a **hero** when you put others first, like handing out water to quench others' thirst.

Ii **Include** other people—
old friends and new.
It's fun to discover
what others can do.

 **Joy** is a feeling
you can show every day.
Just a small smile
can go a long way.

Kk

Be a good friend
and kind without measure.
The friendship you build
is something to treasure.

you'll know you feel **love**
when your heart feels a tug
from a puppy's warm lick
or a sweet grandma's hug.

17

Nn

Doing **nice** things
is always a treat,
like surprising your family
with a room clean and neat.

 **Offer** to help whenever you can. It always feels good giving others a hand.

"Please" is a pleasant way
to request a favor,
like when you ask for ice cream
in your favorite flavor.

Qq

It's fun to laugh loudly,
leaving cares far behind—
but take time each day
to **quiet** body and mind.

Rr

Honor and **respect** creatures big and small. Life is a miracle so treasure it all.

Sometimes it is difficult when you don't want to share, but there's no better way to show someone you care.

Tt

I **trust** that you love me.
I know that you do.
I always feel happy
spending time with you.

Uu

I **understand** you feel sad
when you have a bad day.
yet it helps to know
others feel the same way.

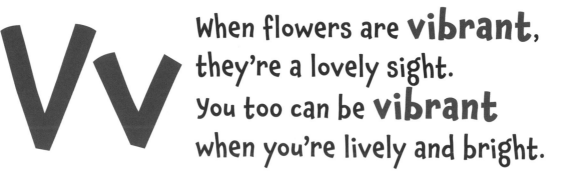

Vv

When flowers are **vibrant**,
they're a lovely sight.
You too can be **vibrant**
when you're lively and bright.

Ww

A **wish** is a dream
you hope will come true,
like wishing for peace
so no one feels blue.

Xx

Be proud of yourself
when you work hard and **excel**.
If you give a strong effort,
you'll always do well.

Yy

Nothing is more amazing than the person who is **you**. You're unique and wonderful. It's absolutely true!

29

When you do things with energy,
you do them with zest.
Stay positive and excited
to give your very best.

Letters make words; this much is true.
There's simply no limit to what words can do.
Using kind words is the place to start,
the kindest of words and the alphabet by heart.

Speak from the heart!